MEMORIES
FROM THE
CLOUD OF LIFE

by

Ray E. Cotnoir

DORRANCE
PUBLISHING CO
EST. 1920
PITTSBURGH, PENNSYLVANIA 15238

Dorrance Publishing Co
585 Alpha Drive
Suite 103
Pittsburgh, PA 15238
Visit our website at *www.dorrancebookstore.com*

ISBN: 978-1-6376-4232-0
eISBN: 978-1-6376-4547-5

MEMORIES
FROM THE
CLOUD OF LIFE

Mother

Rose Cotnoir 1920s

FOREWORD

THERE ARE MULTIPLE PERIODS CONTAINED IN A LIFETIME that hold particular emphasis on experiences which hold differing values for the same individual at different focal points. Consider dividing points as not arbitrary periods of time, but capsules of time involved in reaching an education level, a level of career accomplishments or goals, a time frame for life experiment and evolving change of lifestyle, etc. Pick a name and a period. The memories define the place, events, and participation level of each individual and the social environment affecting the interaction of the players. Capturing the experience in memory is not always true to your feelings at the time.

In my diary of such memoirs, I place emphasis on the strongest attribute required to memorialize fact and communication - the ability to listen and learn - a trait that is a product of education, both formal and social. My cloud contains visual description of the many moments and scenes with family, friends and associates that appear, not necessarily in sequence of time, but as they are called to the stream of memory.

Time frames are spaced by such terms as The Family at Lowell, The School Years at Lowell Graded School, My Experiences at Newport Center High School, The Senior Experience at Aldine, My First Job(s), The Transition to College Life, New Horizons, THE MOVE to Texas, Expanded Horizons, Meeting the Boss, Career Decisions and Professional Experiences, Retirement, My Military Experiences, Our Family in Focus, and Travels.

Throughout these memories is the presence of the character, effect, and drive of my mother who I affectionately refer to as "ROSE." She has been my guiding light in the stressful times of decision making.

Ray Cotnoir's family 1961

INTRODUCTION

CAPTURING MEMORIES OF EARLIER DAYS IS NOT ALWAYS A
sure thing, and it is always influenced by the experiences and
surroundings of interval periods. My reflections of early life
experiences can only be related in capsules of times due to the unusual
times and economic stress that impacted the region of northern Vermont
during the post-depression period through the formation years of the
United Nations.

The area that is today referred to as Northeast Kingdom was then a
relatively under-developed area, mainly engaged in dairy farming and
the entrepreneurial local businesses which were formed to service the
community. The roads were mostly gravel with the exception of those
roads numbered Route 100 —109. Travel was often hampered by
weather and the daily routine chores.

Communication was largely by word of mouth and Bell's multiple-
party line telephone system. The postal service that was centered in a
contract sub-station with rural route delivery. Much of the local information was posted on community information centers at the local general store.

The education system was centered in graded schools (grades 1-8)
and high schools (grades 9-12). Some of the communities had academies,
usually named for the community. A few parochial schools were flour-

ishing as well. There were no "union" or "regional" high schools, but students were transported by bus to centrally located schools to serve the region. I was in such a situation as the town of Lowell contracted with Newport Center High School. This was largely influenced by the terrain and the Route 100 highway system.

Lowell, Vermont, is by area the largest township in the state, centered on the river Missisquoi, which runs north to the Canadian border, finding all the low meadows that harbor the shadows of the Lowell Mountains, Montgomery Notch and Jay Peak to the north and west and the Irasburg Mountains to the east. For all its territorial claim, the town population has not exceeded eight hundred and usually averaged about two-thirds of that number. The town has had different names during its existence. During my years of residence it was composed in population in melting pot formula of English, French Canadian, Irish, and other European descent. Due in part to its proximity to Canada, most of the French townspeople came from Canada's Quebec province, either directly or from Massachusetts which had woolen mills and offered jobs during the Great Depression.

The town's graded school was situated in the Village, a two story wooden building on Route 58, next to St. Ignatius Catholic Church. Two of my teachers, Katherine and Margaret Murphy, were so influential in the lives of their students that the new graded school, now on Route 100, bears their names.

Energy sources during this period had serious limitations. The town's power was produced at a local plant situated on the Missisquoi River in the Lower Village area. That plant was destroyed by the flood of 1936 and electricity as a source of power was not restored until REA arrived after World War II. With the war demands coal and steel were in short supply and not available for heating or energy resources. Natural gas was not placed in the supply pipeline until the 1950s when a pipeline from Maine to Montreal was available in the area. Firewood for the potbelly stoves and furnaces provided heat that could be transferred by pipe to registers with controls installed for public places. A very high premium attached to kerosene for use in lamps and planning for winter wood supply was always a priority in summer months. Many a scar is evident on the arms and legs of wielders of axes and crosscut saws from that era.

Transportation in that time frame was in order of availability, self propulsion, horse and buggy/wagon, automobile, school bus, Vermont Transit Lines; probably airplanes were available but rare in that remote area. Trains were available but only after you used one of the other options.

Resources for individual advancement in achieving goals were then, as now, health, education, resourcefulness, willpower, family support, and faith in one's ability to achieve and surpass expectations. Too often, individual goals could be realized only by moving to a new area of the country. This may account for much of the stagnation in population.

With this backdrop, I introduce you to my early years in my Northeast Kingdom.

Silver Dungeon

CHAPTER 1

GETTING A NEW FAMILY STATUS

 SOME CALL IT A SCENIC RISE AGAINST THE BEAUTY OF A majestic sunset; others call it a restful farm site. My brothers and sisters referred to it as the home place. The current message on the house is "The Silver Dungeon," a vivid description for concrete house that is built below ground level. Such a picture provides for wide variance of sensations that have been experienced at this 32-acre site on Route 58 that at one time bore the title of "The Cotnoir Farm place." I was too young to know any of these emotions at the time the lightning struck and burned to the ground the gathering place and loving home of mother Rose. All of her hard work and stressful endeavors were literally up in smoke. I recall only the ugly view of fire and smoke while being held by my sister trying to keep me out of lightning's and harm's way.

From the ashes of that terrifying night begins a story that bums the words "charity, faith, and hope" in the sky above the Lowell Mountains. It starts with Rose and her commitment to family and her undying faith that no cross is too large or heavy to bear.

From early youth she had experienced problems with her vision. The glasses that enabled her to study and learn English by reading newspapers and community bulletins had grown thicker with each examination. The problem was probably accelerated by the absence of proper lighting in the rental properties which we were forced to live in due to the loss of home and the farm, compounded by the fact that father (a Canadian citizen) was not allowed to return to Vermont due to some alleged illegal activity called smuggling whiskey. Survival had become a key word to the family as the start of WWII brought its government control factors and rations and travel restrictions.

The fire had also done further damage to the family ties. Acting in the interests of the family, the town Selectmen, officials overseeing local cases for charity, had decided the conditions warranted their finding families that could take in the minor girl members of the family. So the three girls soon had new addresses in nearby towns with families which would provide room and board and school access in exchange for the assistance they provided to the "other" families. The three boys, me included, would work for hire, live at home and care for our near blind mother- a seemingly nifty resolution to a community's charitable problem during war time.

By this time the farm had been repossessed to the bank, which later sold it and others at auction. It was not until after the war ended that I revisited the property with visiting relatives from Canada. We were officially on welfare.

The early school years at Lowell Graded were important as that is the point I learned the English language, literally as a foreign language. It seemed a bit unreal to speak French at home, English at school, and the Catholic mass was the Latin mass. Good learning opportunity, to be sure.

The old hotel, converted to an apartment building, served as our early residence. During earlier days the two story structure had housed families of those workers who had operated the dam and power facility in the lower village of Lowell. It was well located at the common area, across from the general store operated by a character named Zen Barnett. The store owner also had an apple orchard and a barn for the twenty jersey dairy cows. It was one of the locations that my brother Gerry and I could work and earn some credit for Rose to get the basic food ingredients for our survival. We could also contribute to sawing and placing blocks of ice, taken from Lake Eden or Lake Memphramegog, in the icehouse adjoining the store. This ice was used to keep refrigerated stored goods in the store and sold to other local commercial users. The ice was covered with sawdust and insulated with heavy burlap cover to prevent melting. We were able to obtain our kerosene for lamps from the Gulf Oil pump outside.

The common area was triangular and maple trees lined the outer limits for the intersections of Route 58 and Route 100. A large gazebo was at its center. To my chagrin, it was the central gathering point for scrap metals during the early years of the war and its beauty was never fully restored.

The house served as a convenient location to school and church. The general store was also a stopping point for the Vermont Transit Lines that would deliver our sisters for school vacations and holidays. Later, during high school years, it was the meeting point for the high school bus. This was home for Rose's family during the years of the "Great War." Excepting the progressive upward movement through the early grades at Lowell Graded, time was suspended by the daily news from the war front, the practice "lights out" sessions in the event of an air raid supervised by the Civilian Air Patrol, and the limited night vision provided by kerosene lamp light.

There were times which allowed Rose to have her family gathered together. I looked forward to the sister visits at Thanksgiving and Christmas. Usually the Transit bus was delayed by snowfall, but there was reward in the musical silence that measured the beat of large snowflakes falling to lay in pure state with other snowflakes. The beauty of the moment led me to research whether or not snowflakes were identical. Not to my surprise, no two are exactly the same. To see the snow flake show against a background of headlights was awesome. It's still my favorite visual memory. It reminds me of the purity of Rose.

Thanksgiving usually evokes thoughts and sensations associated with turkeys. At Rose's family gathering it was a special occasion for the once-a-year roast beef special dinner. That dinner involved home cooked greens, soaked overnight and baked-in-molasses Boston baked beans, bread that had her mark of approval (made from scratch the day before and with yeast added, allowed to rise overnight). The entire dinner was cooked in or on the wood burning stove. Aroma was the essence serving as the dinner bell. The warmth of that special occasion always ended far too soon with my sisters leaving reluctantly to the other appointed family.

The Christmas time visits were different. Great effort was made at the school to involve each student in the spirit of the season. This involved painting the glass windows with Bon Ami colored paste that would stick to the cold glass pane until dry and would capture the wise men, the star and the stable at Bethlehem and the family and surroundings of Jesus. The pageant was always a special production and probably is the most recalled experience of Lowell Graded graduates now that the building is gone. Excitement was abounding at that time of year.

The excitement mounted as days wound to the time of the return family visits of Lorraine, Rita, and Lilly. As they arrived, older brother Gerry and I would search out a "special" spruce tree to be cut, transported by sled, and mounted on a stand that would allow the tree, when erected to be about twelve feet tall. The girls would make some popcorn for stringing, make some paper ornaments and color them, and manipulate some bulbs and icicles. We would have a tree trimming party the afternoon of Christmas Eve. We had no electronic music, but we did have the angelic voice of Rose. Her French singing of the songs of Christmas was singularly enrapturing. She later in life confided to me she had, as a youth, sung solo songs at Cathedral Notre Dame in Montreal. We concluded the Christmas Eve preparation by walking to St Ignatius Church to sing carols and participate in The Midnight Mass. When concluded, we plodded back up the hill to the "house on the commons" for hot chocolate and a well deserved night's rest.

As a family without a breadwinner, a mother nearing blindness, no independent means of improving our situation, there was seemingly all possibilities for frequent or even permanent disillusion and trauma. While others were opening Christmas gifts from family and friends, we were sharing in the welfare package distribution. I must say, the blue winter coat I received in the winter of 1943 probably kept me from a bout with frostbite. While others would share the upgrades and latest goods, we received the gift of a strong faith and strengthening will of mother Rose. The light that shone from those eyes that couldn't see led the way and marked the path for each of us to follow.

Lorraine was now old enough to be employed and she started work in a military plant at Burlington; Rita was studying to be a nurse and doing part time work at restaurants; Lillian was graduating with honors at Bakersfield; and Gerry is now ready for high school at Newport Center. Gerry and I have now a job before and after school of tending a herd of dairy cattle at the Dugan farm on Irish Hill in Lowell. The pay is equivalent of the bus fare to ride the High School bus the eighteen miles to Newport Center High School for Gerry, and we were able to keep out enough milk for mother and three boys. Mr. Dugan was the superintendent of schools and would later play a key role for Gerry to receive a scholarship at the University of Vermont. My younger brother, Roger, is now in school and is eight years old. The war is ending in Europe; I am starting to see a wider horizon.

CHAPTER 2

THE GREAT DEPRESSION HAD BEEN PRECEDED BY PROHI-bition. Vermont was positioned strategically between the cities of the east and the province of Quebec, which held no sympathy with those who enforced prohibition laws and rules. Opportunity met need on many occasion to skirt those rules. Smuggling of foreign whiskey or illegally processed alcohol led many a daredevil to choose opportunity over safety to enhance the family income. Antoine, husband of Rose and father of their six children, allegedly fell into the trap. Smuggler's notch was within range of the family farm.

Born in Three Rivers, P. Q. made him a citizen of Canada. Although Rose was born in the state of Massachusetts, she had deep roots in Canada. Rose Girouard married Antoine Cotnoir in August, 1923, in St-Victoire, P. Q., Canada. They moved to Massachusetts and three children and six years later were able to purchase the farm on Route 58 in Lowell, Vermont. Their three sons, Gerry, myself, and Roger, were born in Lowell. The Depression hit everyone a massive blow and forced the men to go elsewhere to work at odd jobs.

Logging was widespread in the northeast part of Vermont. The Missisquoi River provided a way to float the logs to saw mills up river toward Canada. The waterfalls at North Troy were especially dangerous and many a mishap ended the careers of the workers herding the logs through the rough waters. Hazardous pay was definitely in order for those brave workers. The route to open transportation paralleled the Canadian border for several miles on the river, enabling opportunity for illegal transfer of alcohol to take place in a ready-made work place.

Antoine's problems with the border patrol and the alcohol and tobacco division of the Department of Treasury soon became a force which led to the barring of entry to the U.S. from Canada. Complicating the right of appeal for Antoine was the bad temper which was on display when he consumed the alcohol.

There are differing ways for a husband to display abuse. Although no physical abuse was involved, his failing to recognize the primary responsibility to his wife and children was not only neglectful, but also abusive. The penalty was for him to be tested and sent for treatment at the Waterbury, Vermont, institution, where Rose could occasionally visit him in hopes that all would resolve to their reunion. When released from treatment, he was returned to Canada and barred from reentry to the states.

As a boy, I recall one occasion at Lowell during which I was chastised for not eating green olives and instructed by him to leave the dinner table. It was snowing outside, so I joined a neighbor friend in some low slope ski jumping on skis that we had made from old barrel staves. This episode is the only real memory of my personal relationship with Antoine, my father.

The effects of World War II in the European area had a large impact on the Town of Lowell. Most of the able bodied young men were called or enlisted in the country's military service. For me and my brothers, it was a time to grow in service that served the community while enabling us to distance ourselves from the plight we had been handed by Antoine's condition and position. School played a large part of the early growth and expansion of our horizons as the war news brought the sobering and oft times tragic telegrams explaining the losses of the area's most able young men.

The period from grades 4-8 was a collection of "episodes" that bear review. There was speculation that the mile long strip of land on Route 100 which was the longest stretch of flatland in the northern area would somehow become a landing strip for use by the Civil Air Patrol and corresponding military planes. Thankfully that never materialized and the Village was left intact. Of considerable concern for the town was the war effort to gather all matter of scrap metals from haying equipment to motor engines to wheel rims off of wagons and place them all in the town common which was the center of the Town of Lowell. As well intentioned as the effort seemed, the resulting mountain of rusted metals was a terrible eyesore for months before removal. It did cause the community to clean up the Missisquoi River and local tributaries for the decade. I recall two important personal thoughts, the removal of a large motor from the waterfall in the Lower Village area on which I lost numerous fishing lines, and secondly, the broken arm suffered by the father of my best friend while unloading a side windrow rake. He was the person hauling the area farms' milk to the creamery at Newport for which he was disabled for some time.

The "blackout" drills which were called for were usually during the time I had available for the reading and school homework assignments. With wick light from kerosene lamps it was doubtful that enough light was available to penetrate the curtains that were closed.

During these difficult times, Rose had learned to read English from various newspapers. We were able to scrape through the cold winters with ration stamps and vegetables she canned and fruits preserved from neighboring apple orchards. Gerry and I were able to come away with wholesome milk as part of our payment for the chores performed at the "Dugan" farm before and after school. I had started an outbreak of measles when in the fourth grade and our family home was quarantined for two weeks. I was relieved that the quarantine was lifted just in time for the first day of trout season, May 1, 1944. It snowed that day, but, true to the sport and my love of it, the result was a limit catch. All too soon school and another end of school year parade to the picnic ground (now called "Gelo Park") came around Memorial Day and the long summer months of working in the hay field ensued.

Hitching up two horses to a hay wagon was an early life experience. The two work horses were Morgan horses and given the hilly terrain with side hill valleys, the challenge was always to keep the load properly balanced to avoid losing the load. I learned to space tumbles of hay apart and place a binding pitch fork of hay to secure the loading of larger middle tumbles as levelers.

All of this was done under the watchful eye of neighbor Zen Barnett. So, too, was the wide turn required to keep the wagon load from over turning. The men pitching the hay were not always accurate with their pitch and, on occasion, caused me to lose balance and fall from the wagon. This experience was an early life indicator of the balance needed to deal with later life surprises.

The converted hotel, which had previously been the housing for employees and families that manned the power plant at the waterfall on Highway 58 in the lower village, was our place of apartment residence at the end of WWII. It was the gathering place of Rose's family for those special occasions at Thanksgiving and Christmas. It was located at the common, the joining of Route 100 and Vermont 58, stood four stories tall and had wide and sturdy staircases. The "apartment" had a high ceiling. Maple trees of grand stature were directly outside and outlined the triangular commons that was frequently our playground. The general store owned by Mrs. Sweet, managed by Zen Barnett, was a central gathering place for persons living in the Upper Village. It was the place of card games that I learned as a youth that still stir fond memories. The storage garage building next to the apartment had been reduced to ground level and was uncovered. During some of the major snow events it was a hazard that found me in snow above my head on occasion for walking too closely to the perimeter.

As time passed, my memory marked several occasions which served to notch heroism and dedication as mother Rose's character. Her dedication to the children and the education in the public schools despite her loss of sight and language barrier were exemplary. Her strong adherence to religious principles was evident in all the hours of her day. She started each morning with God at her helm through morning prayers, we thanked Him for the food we were able to secure, grow or capture, and the night ended with bedtime prayers. Although we spoke English, we prayed in French. Often times she would sing to us in French. I think the victory garden that produced our vegetables and fruit were especially productive due to our needs and her prayers. She believed that all things within our power to effect would materialize if properly pursued. It is truly remarkable how much of our needs were provided for with so little income.

One remarkable Christmas brought oldest sister, Lorraine, to visit from her location at the city of Burlington. She was accompanied by a future brother-in-law, Frank. This was a time in life when a young boy starts to question the image and reality of Santa Claus. As I had an aspiration to play the part of an engineer, the Erector set that Frank had arranged was responsible for seeing me through the troubled times of doubting Santa. I forgot totally to look for the sleigh marks on the roof. Later that week, after the new wore off the Erector set, the part of me that researched law asserted itself and I was convinced that mine was a future in dealing with contracts, not erection of structures. Frank had in one short meeting guided me to my guiding light. From that point forward, I had a hankering to become engaged with law.

Almost all of life's critical decisions are the product of the environment surrounding us, the influence of outside mentors, and our ability to weigh the issues that balance our judgments. Rose added the main ingredient which was in our family presence daily. She was inspirational by her example of tenacity to cope with hardships; she was strong in her persuasion that the easy way was not necessarily the proper way, she adhered to a strong allegiance to prayer and the power of goodness and hope. Whenever a decision was to be reached, guidance was within reach. Given that support no dream was too remote to chase and the imagination conjured up many scenarios for future direction. Imagination is a real source of direction, even if the road to success is narrowed by dangers along the way. Boot straps were always within reach and if properly used would help raise you and your sights higher.

CHAPTER 3

LIVING IN THE LOWER VILLAGE BROUGHT NEW ACQUAINTANCES, new challenges, and a different outlook. As a boy of eleven years, school was now becoming filled with events. The end of the War was within sight for America. Social changes brought about by social security enactment were in evidence. A strong energy was evident in the schools now that more certainty could be had as to the economic influence of peace. Returning from the military, the hardened soldiers showed both the joy and relief from battle fatigue and the trauma of returning to the civilian stage of life. Each town and village had its private "Peyton Place;" Lowell was no different.

I was a very proud uncle at age eleven as sister Lorraine presented her son to husband Frank and the Lowell Cotnoir family. I could not have been more moved than when I announced to the villagers that Dudley Gaylord Hale was a healthy baby boy. It was as though I had somehow grown considerably older overnight. A large rock had been removed from overhead and somehow sunshine penetrated those dark and cold January days, and it became apparent to me that she had more than a little concern about the marriage but was a real soldier of Christ in the birth of her first grandson. Prayer had always been a sundial for her day, but she was in continual contact with the Lord over his most recent blessing. There was an air of excitement which carried into the miserably cold month of February.

Some periods of time are memorialized by unusual events. On the occasions that January temperatures rose to the freezing mark, snow would melt at the warm peak times of early afternoon. As the sun started over the tall peaks at Mount Norris and the range north to Jay Peak, the warmth of the sun would turn to a chilling and bitter cold late afternoon and cause ice to form from the moistened snow and roadways would freeze in place so that the crunching of tires or sleds or footsteps on the surface would penetrate the early night air. The metal pails we used to fetch water from the spring would be our way to break the surface of the ice cover, allowing us to fill the pail with ice water to bring to the house for heating over the wood stove. Bathing would require that several pails of water be gathered and heated in this manner. Wood burning meant wood cutting and wood splitting during the early summer months so that it could dry and furnish a smokeless fire in the two stoves, one in the kitchen area, the other in the living area. Cords and cords of home grown wood from the trees were needed. Coal, coke, and other fuels were not available until the late '40's due to the war effort.

During this winter, brother Roger and I would skate on the icy surface of the two rivers that merged at the whirlpool bend in the Missisquoi River. One late January day as the sun warmed the afternoon temperature to twenty degrees above zero we took our sleds, skates, mufflers, and hats to the confluence of the rivers about a quarter mile from the home. We started to clear the surface of snow and check the ice thickness for safety. Roger ventured too near the current and the ice broke pulling him into the icy waters where he immediately became immobilized and a victim of shock. I was able to free him from the current and place him on the sled, cover him with the coats and clothing available and, with strength from adrenaline and divine intervention, get him to the road, up the hill and to the house. Fortunately, Lorraine was still at home and we were able to get him out of the icy clothing, into a tub of cold water and gradually warm it to bring him out of shock and place him in some blankets. I never pass by that whirlpool without revisiting that very fortunate day. I was fortunate to not have been a factor in causing Rose to lose her youngest son, Pierre Roger, whom she had charged me with protecting. I know that a few of the prayers from her prayer bank were in use that cold afternoon.

Soon after this event, Frank was free from the army and employed at a printing company in Waterbury, a place that held only fringe memories to me of my father's presence in a state managed mental facility. Lorraine and their new baby, Dudley, joined him in their home at Waterbury. An interval passed before the introduction of son number two, Frank George Hale, reached the distant town of Lowell - distant only because of the mountainous terrain and limited communication facilities. Life in this remote region had accelerated in speed due to the rapid sequence of change that followed the end of World War II in August, 1945. In the months following, Frank had an opportunity to pursue a larger and better position with a printing company in Texas; he, and later Lorraine and the boys, moved to Houston.

Sister Rita was employed and in training to be a nurse at White River Junction and Burlington in these times of the late 1940's. While at Burlington she met and later married an engineering student at UVM. I recall that was my first experience at attending a wedding. I wore a white shirt, coat, and tie for my very first time to be at a wedding, which was held as a nuptial mass in the Catholic Church on Church Street in Burlington. That city seemed like a metropolis at the time. The event ended all too sudden for me as we returned to the house in Lowell following the reception at the South Burlington Howard Johnson Restaurant where both Rita and Bunny had waited on tables.

Lillian, or "Bunny" as she became known had made her way to the UVM campus where she excelled as an honor student and brought honors in numerous ways through her many achievements, graduating as a member of the Mortar Board Society. Her qualifications earned an op-

portunity to be an interpreter at the initial convention of the United Nations; however, she chose to accept a commission in the Women's Army
Corps following her graduation. In several ways, this provided a better
way forward for Rose as her eyesight was greatly diminished. She was
eligible for further assistance as a dependent mother which allowed her
greater mobility and income.

As each summer brought differing farm locations for me to herd
cows, do chores, and learn the farming system, I became more resolute
in the decision I had reached to study hard, do as well as possible in high
school and find an avenue to the path of attending college as did Bunny
and, later, Gerry. Gerry and I were brothers in more ways than just having a same bloodline. We had become the head of Rose's home. Gerry
was a very strong young man with a wonderful wit about him. It was
easy to see and follow the ways that he used in preparing for challenges.

He had the strength to deal with adversity of all kinds. He would
often tell me that mother's eyesight loss was incurable but she was so
dedicated in prayer that miracles could provide other avenues for her to
experience travel, technology, and the rewards of sharing her guiding
light with others. Maybe that was what inspired me to expand her knowledge of the game of baseball.

I had been given a radio that had tubes and was a discard and a challenge to use as a crystal radio. Just the thought of being able to bring
sounds of voices and music into the house inspired me to work on that
little device and somehow I managed to get the early morning refrains of
a radio station in Wheeling, West Virginia Station WWVA. It had mountain country and blue grass music and on weekends carried live the
sounds of the WWVA Jamboree. This early success caused me to search
for some station that would bring a daily break in the life of mother. Enter
the Soap series "Un home et son peches," "A man and his sins," from the
radio Canada station in Montreal. During baseball season, the effort
switched to night baseball games. The strongest radio signal was WMGM

New York, which carried the games of the Brooklyn Dodgers. I became a Dodger die-hard fan and was annually disappointed that they could not beat the Yankees in the World Series. That enthusiasm somehow caused Rose to also listen to the games, but since she didn't understand the game, she needed to ask a lot of questions.

The Town of Lowell men had a team that was in a league composed of teams in the Northeast Kingdom. My brother Gerry and I tried out for positions on the local team. Initially only Gerry made the team as I was deemed too young and small to play against mature young men. On occasion I would take our nearly blind mother to watch the local home games that would be played in a field that is now designated as Gelo Park. She was able to get an understanding of the basic game and rules of baseball in this setting so she could translate and visualize the sounds of the Dodger games as narrated by the voice of the Dodgers, Red Barber. She became a real fan of baseball and would often fall asleep with the radio still playing.

About the time of my freshman year at Newport Center High Gerry had been selected to be in an advanced "honors" position in NCHS which required that he live in Newport Center during school days and he did chores and roomed at the small farm of the math teacher, Ms. Briggs, who was a wonderful but demanding algebra teacher. This enabled Gerry to also play on the High School basketball team under coach and principal, Wally Martin. The team had not enjoyed a lot of success during those war years, but Gerry and his team mates soon altered the trend. Soon the Newport Center "Blue Devils" would compete for District honors and tournament competition. This meant little to the Town of Lowell but was a milestone in the maturing of the Cotnoir boys. I took a real interest in competitive sports and looked forward with anxiety to the beginning of each fall. The control of teams was especially effective as the coach was Wally Martin, the principal and also the team bus driver for games. Away games were especially challenging in the cold of winter months. So, too, was the challenge for Rose as we were gone for extended hours and she would then be dependent upon younger brother, Roger, to do the chores that followed school hours. She never complained, but many were the nights I felt guilt in my enjoyment of the bus ride home knowing that in a few short hours I would be up at dawn and catching that same buss back to Newport Center.

During the early days of my freshman year as a Blue Devil, the usual hazing pranks were handed out by the super sophomores and I was dressed in long johns over my clothes with winter boots as my dress code. The trauma and humiliation of such ridiculous dress as a classroom participant was enough to slice and dice my ego for weeks. Compounding that feeling was the horror of being told to sit in my chair that had been filled with water. I soon lost my star struck aura and realized that the real discipline of high school years is in your ability to withstand ridicule and move on to the next important issues in life. Those issues kept on coming.

Basketball was the main event in the schools of the Northeast Kingdom. Football was for the "big city" high schools and the only one in our area was Newport High. Most of the boys in basketball had daily farm duties and practices had to be a part of physical education class and individual workouts as the time was available. In the first year we utilized the small hall adjacent with the two story high school building and did wind sprints from end to end, all of fifty feet. The baskets were flush with the walls on ends and the sidelines were the side walls. Numerous rib injuries were encountered in the tough practices and spacing for shots was non-existent. Finally, Coach Martin persuaded the Superintendant that we should have access to the National Guard Armory in Newport for games and later practices. Out of that formula came some pretty good teams and competition in our league.

As a freshman, it was improbable that I should get extended playing time on the court. Although I was short and a lightweight, speed and vision were gifts that allowed me that opportunity to play. I recall the early reminder that occurred on a brutally cold January night in a game in Island Pond with Brighton High. Flashing some of the speed and "quick hands" of a Bob Cousy, I tied up the center for a jump ball. As I attempted to tip the ball, he turned his hip into my chest, knocking me to the hardwood floor where his 6'5" body landed on my head. After a few rounds of smelling salts, and being lifted from the floor to a seat on the sidelines, I realized that one tooth was broken and one cracked, and the broken tooth had probably been swallowed. The exposed nerve of the broken tooth was more excruciating than the view of my teeth missing the two top front teeth, Concussion was probably an additional injury. I am convinced that the alternating possession rule for jump balls stemmed from similar accidents. To add to the torment, the minus twenty degree outside temperature made for a very long and miserably painful ride on the bus back to Lowell. Brother Gerry chided me for being a wimp which was an issue between us until I realized that sports participation carries with it risk commensurate with reward. Several dentists became the beneficiaries of the repair job.

The cold winter nights of late January caused an eerie but beautiful morning scene as I looked east at sunrise. I often checked the temperature on the mercury thermometer on the front porch. The coldest morning that I recorded was at seven A.M. when the thermometer, which went to minus sixty degrees had the mercury break through its bottom. No school that day!

CHAPTER 4

NEW HORIZONS WERE APPEARING WITH EACH PASSING month after the end of World War II. The return of veterans was a signal of change in the area as fewer men were willing to take up the challenge of returning to the farm as a way of life. There was a decided need for change in both the scope of personal development and the range of travel and relocation of young people resulting in large part to the influence of veteran programs for advanced education and professional training programs. This led to relocation of families or family members. In Rose's family alone, Lorraine and Frank moved to Houston, Rita met Doug and following college and the Korean conflict, they moved to other parts of Vermont and then to Florida, Washington, California, and Arizona with an expanding family. Lillian joined the WAC and moved around the country until meeting her Air Force husband and moving from Air Force Base to Air Force Base until Jim's tour ended. Gerry had been in the Air Force ROTC at UVM which carried with it an obligation to accept a commission after college and he was off to Kansas where he met and married Donna.

I was an enigma in that Mother, Roger, and I moved from Lowell to be in Houston where, in 1951, Roger and I enrolled at Aldine High school upon arrival on a Labor Day weekend. Culture shock could not adequately describe the experience. That first day was the warmest temperature I had experienced in my lifetime. The sun seemed like a large red rock suspended on the horizon with impending threat to roll down the landscape and crush all in its way. This experience followed our travel from the sixty degree day in Lowell and travel to Burlington where we caught the midnight sleeper to New York City passing Yankee Stadium enroute to Grand Central station. We taxied to New York's Henry Hudson Hotel where we stayed daytime until it was time to return to Grand Central Station and board a bus to Newark International Airport across the New York Skyway. We had walked to a restaurant, Hamburger Heaven, and saw some local sights including St. Patrick's Cathedral. Time did not permit me to accept the invitation of a family at the hotel to accompany them for a tour of the Queen Mary that was moored in New York Harbor. This tour came fifty-five years later at the stationary location at Long Beach, California.

Roger returned briefly to Vermont from Houston with Rose and he left high school during his final year to join the U.S. Army during the Korean War days and was a six year enlistee spending much of that time in the Pacific Theatre.

After I returned briefly to Vermont during July of 1952, I enrolled at UVM as a freshman and that lasted until the first blizzard around early November, at which time I withdrew from UVM and traveled back to Houston by Greyhound Bus over a three day span. Renewing old friendships sparked a new appreciation of the area as I regained my job at Henke-Pilot Stores. The redetermination to earn a college degree shifted to a path at Texas A&M University. My enrollment there in January,1953, entailed being in the Corps of Cadets in the Air Force ROTC. At semester's end I went to Dallas where sister Lorraine and her family resided.

The full time summer job was in the proximate area of SMU and I became familiar with the campus and its rich traditions. In late 1953 I applied for transfer of my work at Texas A&M to SMU and applied for admission to the Dallas based university. With acceptance the path to a degree seemed assured. It is at this stage of my life that I truly felt a sense of maturity settling into my daily routine. Self-dependence was a trait that required daily attention and planning so that a long-term plan could evolve and short-term achievements would not be crushed. Fortunately I had the strong example in the person of Rose to steer course my direction and follow the difficult path of adhering to planned goals.

CHAPTER 5

AN UNUSUAL ROAD TO SUCCESS

THE ROAD OF LIFE IS TRAVELLED WITH DIFFERENT GATES for different folks. Often times the key influence in direction is not really within the sight line of the individual. Plans for the future can literally be changed by a temporary response or a so-called "good deed" in a normal day's routine.

On January 23, 1956, I was busy doing homework during a study period in my room at the fraternity house. One of the brothers came to me and relayed his story of becoming a volunteer to enlist in the U.S. Army. George's close friend from Long Island, new York, had been killed in a charge at the battle line in the Korean Conflict. His reaction was to "go get some revenge" and he had reacted with this emotion to join the army.

George had a part time job in Dallas' business district that called for him to do some service work in a mail room before classes, return in the afternoon to assemble the outgoing mail and contract packaging, and deliver the mail to the main postal facility. Handling the printing of payroll reports by mimeograph operations could be done in slack times, after normal work hours, or on Saturday. George was leaving the next morning for induction and processing and didn't want to spring the news of his departure without offering a solution to his employer. I agreed to offer to help until the USF&G could find a replacement.

Enter stage left, I called the manager to arrange an interview to take the role for the time required to find a suitable replacement and keep George's record clear for not having given the two week notice. This was my introduction to the business world environment. The manager accepted me and made the arrangements for me to meet travel and class time requirements. The employer liked my responses to their needs and when they didn't receive any applicants by full time workers for the job, asked for me to continue on and made a proposal to extend the job as a full time part time position until my school year end and beyond. That was my introduction to the business world.

As semesters came and went, the work became more easily managed. It helped that the regional manager was a lawyer and, my course of study being pre-law enabled me to learn some of the legal decisions common to the financial, construction, and insurance business community. I had the opportunity to look over the mail associated with a wide range of decisions, arguments, and the structure of the decision making process.

So the pavement to the business world had a light with a guide and soon the exposure to the fabric and framework of the company/agency relationship in the business of insurance and surety was a part of my daily life. The company was proactive in the training of young persons entering the field of underwriting, engineering, and claims. The opportunity to select a career to become a professional with career objectives was a distinct possibility to consider as college degree work advanced.

As time passed during that year, I became captured by the many facets of dealing with construction contractors, the several professions that engaged them and the contracts they bid, reviewed, acquired, and performed. The framework of construction, the relations with awarding authorities, the funding to pay for work, the labor relations with unions, the negotiations with banks, subcontractors and suppliers - all brought into focus just how broad a spectrum was involved in bringing the architects' plans and the engineers specifications into a completed building, road, dam, bridge, etc. that dots our wonderful country. The prospect of being engaged in that process as a profession appealed to me. My employer, USF&G, was a leader in many areas relating to surety and fidelity bonding.

As I accrued a secure relationship with this employer, I was able to relinquish the other part time jobs that had enabled my college work to progress and reach a senior year level. I continued to reside at the PIKE house and enjoyed the occasional opportunity to take in college football and basketball games at the Cotton Bowl and Moody Coliseum. Social life mainly surrounded the fraternity parties and member organizations on campus.

In late '56 I was introduced to a young woman, a sophomore at North Texas State College, Sybil Fain, and over the holidays we dated a couple of times. I introduced her to maple sugar candies from Vermont. In the following spring we became a steady weekend date, sharing visits to her sorority and my fraternity parties. I gave her a frat pin. As summer approached, we agreed to be engaged. Somehow, in my move to an apartment, I forgot to send a notice of changed address to my Vermont draft board at St. Albans where I registered at age eighteen.

My brother, Gerry, was an officer in the Air Force, stationed in Morocco. He called on a military line to advise that my draft board contacted him to find my location. After I called them the following day, I was aware that my classification was changed from deferred to 1A. Fortunately for me my neighbor in the apartment was a Senior MSgt at the Naval Air Station and he arranged for me to visit the personnel officer the following day. That day I was advised of openings in the Texas ANG and I was accepted and sworn in, with a delayed date for basic training at San Antonio, delayed until November/December. I was again blessed in that USF&G not only blessed the ANG but would pay me for the active duty time I was required to participate without losing paid vacation.

Sybil and I were married on Friday the 13th of September as the last couple to be married at the mission church of the St. Augustine Parish in Dallas. All my life's "loose ends" had been bundled up in one summer, so I thought. You know, the only difference would be "one more mouth to feed." I still had a lot to learn and it came fast.

I had, during the summer of '57, been interviewed by each of the underwriting managers, and offered a choice by the manager, a choice of underwriting departments, and I selected the fidelity/surety department. and would be designated as a home office trainee. It was a one year on-the-job training program with written guides and monthly progress reports and exams, under the supervision of a genuine citizen for the ages, Mr. Frank Grafflin. He was an attorney, a judicial expert, having attended law school in Maryland while working in the home office of the company. He travelled the country, working as their examiner of judicial court cases. He wrote a book on the subject of court and fiduciary bonds that had the status of the "Bible" for bond underwriters in probate and court cases of civil and criminal matters. He was thorough in all matters legal and thought of his employees as family members. His motto was "BE HERE, BE ON TIME, BE TRUTHFUL, AND RESPECT YOUR FELLOW EMPLOYEES." He would see that you did your job. How can that message not be successful? During one of his judicial visits to probate court in Fannin County, Texas, he met and later married his wife, Irene. I considered it a privilege to call him mentor and friend.

Lackland Air Force Base was then an assembly of Quanset Huts, all in a row, with rows of numbers, a mess hall, a bunch of parade grounds, a paymaster window, and a mail room. I am sure there were other more desirable places on base, but, in basic training the day began at five A.M. and ended in the dark of November and December nights. No time off for holidays as they brought guard and KP duty. I was in a squadron largely composed of ANG personnel from Texas, the Midwest plains, and a large group from New York state. I had previously had a "butch"

Ray and Wife in 1967

haircut so the humiliating experience on day two of arrival didn't destroy my idea of discipline. My barracks sergeant, SMSgt Stephens, had served in both WWII and Korea and knew all the ways to anoint you as a dummy. About fifty percent had college background, so we were somewhat prepared for the "ninety day wonder" tour. In all ways except how to treat rumors, that is. It seemed that the last week of the tour had us leaving early, going to the regular Air Force, almost anything but being sent back to our ANG unit. Ninety days to the day, I caught the bus back to Dallas. I had a better physical stature for having been there, but was thrilled to be reunited with Sybil and returned to work at USF&G the following week. During my stay at San Antonio I became acquainted with fellow guardsman, Bob Young, and our paths would keep us and our wives in close friendship until this day.

Shortly after return I again enrolled in college courses and resumed the completion of degree work but mostly at night courses in deference to the requirement of full time OJT. We lived in a house on Binkley Street, in Highland Park until spring when we moved into a duplex in East Dallas.

As the months passed and the "trainee" program became meshed with compounded duties at the office I became more fully aware of the expanding horizon of the legal practice and its relationship with surety and fidelity and the decision making process. For all the excitement and detail, the finality of an underwriting decision was the true test of my willingness to look at the career aspect of that path as a road to success.

EPILOGUE

as adapted to my 1963 poem,
"To the Sea"

ALL ELEMENTS ARE PLACED RELATION TO ONE ANOTHER so that order and renewal of energy will continually balance nature. Like the flow of water from snow capped mountains to streams, to rivers, to lakes, To oceans that evaporate and renew the process, so is the element of knowledge as it is placed in relation to other thoughts and verses and books to flow toward the seas of universal knowledge

Knowledge is bundled ideas that may grow or be modified through discussion, research, debate, through silence. Simple ideas are never as simple as they appear. Thorough knowledge is an accumulation of simple ideas modified through discussion. Problems are solved by a flow of to complex ideas.

The flow of ideas in the information stream seems more silent in the river based upon the distance you are from the central current. Ice forms more quickly in still or slow moving waters. Awareness of the debris that collects in a whirlpool is vital to keep the clear stream of ideas flowing through nature. The more an idea is washed, the more clarity of sight and sound. water is filtered clear of foam after its deafening roar over a waterfall. So it is, also, with the sounds of debate; the more discussion, the clearer the resolution.

Life is the sum of your experiences with the knowledge assimilated by education, both formal and in the universal family experience. Balance and dedication to both are rewarding, the challenge is great, the seas are placid.

Ray Lake Tahoe

The Ancient Arms of

Cotnoir

auphin was not one of the original founding states of France. Nestled in the Rhone Valley and the picturesque Alps, Dauphin was a part of the Holy Roman Empire. It is from this area that the surname Cotnoir is believed to have originated.

Traditionally the province was administered by the Counts of Vienna who were the ruling house. In the 5th century the Burgondes controlled the region but the Franks overran the domain as they did most of France. The region was later contested by the Merovingians and the Carolingians. They were later integrated into the kingdom of Provence and then into the second kingdom of Provence which was Bourgogne. It was not until 1391 that Dauphin became an integral part of the Kingdom of France. The family name Cotnoir was first found in Dauphiné where this celebrated family were seated since ancient times.

Most surnames have experienced slight spelling changes. A son may not choose to spell his name the same way that his father did. Many were errors, many deliberate. Usually a person gave his version, phonetically, to a scribe, a priest, or a recorder. Prefixes or suffixes varied. They were optional as they passed through the centuries, or were adopted by different branches to signify either a political or religious adherence. Hence, we have variations in your name, Cotnoir some of which are Cochet, Cocher, Cochez, Coché, Cochée, Cochait, Cochait, Cochaies, Cochey, Cochest, Cochais, Cuchet, Cauchy, Cuchet, Cuché, Cuchez, Cucher, Cuchest, Cuchait, Cuchais, Cochette to distinguish but a few.

In the llth century Guigues the First, Lord of Albon acquired the centre of Dauphin by conquest. He acquired a part of Vienna, the main and capital city. In 1162, the Lords of Bourgogne succeeded to the Lords of Albon, and they were followed by the Lords of the Tour de Pin in 1281. This latter group was known as the first Lords of Dauphin and gave their name to the region.

In 1349, Hubmert II, without heirs, left his possessions to the King of France under the treaty with the Romans. The condition of this treaty was that the eldest Prince of France, that is, the Crown Prince, would always bear the title of 'The Dauphin'. Dauphin then became an integral part of the Kingdom of France.

The family name Cotnoir was found in Dauphiné where the family were seated with lands and manors. Alexandre Cuchet is mentioned in 1669 as the Master of Teil and his daughter, Marie Cuchet, married François Massis, a Lawyer and a Doctor. According to the marriage contract, their children carried on the Cuchet name hyphenated to the Massis name. Many members of this family became prominent citizens in their regions, holding important political positions and controlling much land. A distinctive member of the family was Pierre Massis-Cuchet, a Lawyer, who became the perpetual Mayor of Teil during the 1700's. Marie Cochet du Magny was a counsellor in the Court of Inquiry in 1763. The French Revolution and its resultant political and social upheaval involved many families, including the Cochet's Henri Louis Joseph Cochet was elected a Deputy to the Legislature on August 29, 1791, and was re-elected in 1792 as a member of the Convention where he voted for the death of the King. For his support, Bonaparte named him a Judge at the Criminal Tribunal. Notable amongst the family at this time was Pierre Massis-Cuchet, Lawyer and perpetual Mayor of Teil.

During the early 16th century in France there was an expanding awareness of European leadership. Exploration of the New World became a

challenge. Following the explorers along the eastern seaboard of North America, settlements included, from north to south, New France, followed by New England, New Holland, and New Spain.

Jacques Cartier made the first of three voyages to New France in 1534. The Jesuits, Champlain in 1608, and the Church missionaries, followed. In general, the plans for developing Quebec fell far short of the objectives of the Company of New France. Champlain made over twenty voyages to France in order to encourage immigration to New France. The first true migrant, Louis Hebert, a Parisian apothecary, and his family, arrived in 1617.

In 1643, 109 years after the first landings by Cartier, there were only about 300 people in Quebec, in 1663 there were only 500, 2,000 migrants arrived during the next decade. Early marriage was desperately encouraged amongst the immigrants. Youths of 18 took fourteen year old girls for their wives.

The fur trade was developed and attracted migrants, both noble and commoner from France. 15,000 explorers left Montreal in the late 17th and 18th centuries. Migration from France to New France or Quebec as it was now more popularly called, continued from France until it fell in 1759. By 1675, there were 7000 French in Quebec. By the same year the Acadian presence in Nova Scotia, New Brunswick and Prince Edward Island had reached 500. In 1755, 10,000 French Acadians refused to take an oath of allegiance to England and were deported to Louisiana. Meanwhile, in Quebec, the French race flourished, founding in Lower Canada, one of the two great solitudes which became Canada.

Amongst the settlers in North America with this distinguished name Cotnoir were Charles B. P. Cochet settled in Philadelphia in 1806, André Cochet settled in Virginia in 1700; Georg Dietrich Cochet settled in Philadelphia in 1768; Isaac Cochet settled in Philadelphia in 1768; Heanne Susan Cochet settled in America in 1753; Johan Isaac Cochet settled in Philadelphia in 1768, Rachel Cochet settled in Philadelphia in 1751.

Settlers began to increasingly look westward, as opportunities arose. In America, the Homestead Act (1862) offered 160 acres of land for a minimal fee; while in Canada, the Dominion Lands Act (1872) offered 160 acres to any male over the age of 21 for a ten-dollar registration fee.

Many distinguished contributions have been made by members of this family name Cotnoir. It has been prominent in the arts, religion, politics and culture in France and New France; Yves Cochet, French politician; Henri Cochet (1901–1987), French tennis player; Baron Augustin Louis Cauchy, French mathematician.

The coat of arms found for a bearer of the Cotnoir surname did not include a motto. Under most heraldic authorities, a motto is an optional component of the coat of arms, and many families have chosen not to display a motto.

Family Crest

CPSIA information can be obtained
at www.ICGtesting.com
Printed in the USA
BVHW022257050921
615877BV00001B/1